D1348994

Instant Expert

MOTOCROSS
SKILLS

Anthony Sutton

A & C BLACK

Published by:
A & C Black
Bloomsbury Publishing Plc
49–51 Bedford Square
London WC1B 3DP

www.acblack.com

First published 2011
Copyright © 2011 Bloomsbury Publishing Plc

Original concept: Paul Mason
Project management: Paul Mason
Design: Mayer Media

ISBN   HB 9781408147221
          PB 9781408147214

A CIP record for this book is available from the
British Library.

This book is produced using paper made from
wood grown in managed, sustainable forests.
It is natural, renewable, and recyclable. The
logging and manufacturing processes conform
to the environmental regulations of the
country of origin.

Printed and bound in Malaysia by
Tien Wah Press

Photo acknowledgements:
All interior photos © Anthony Sutton
Cover: main image © Alain Cimon
Photography, all others Shutterstock.

WARNING!
**Motocross training is dangerous and
should be undertaken only under
the supervision of a trained instructor.
Readers should never attempt to
undertake the techniques
described in this book without the
supervision of such an instructor.**

**Always wear complete safety gear while
riding, including a helmet, chest protector,
boots and pads.**

**The authors and publishers of this book
assume no legal or financial responsibilty,
either direct or implied, that may result
from the use, abuse, or misuse of the
information contained herein.**

Contents

Why become a
motocross
expert?

Get the low-down on becoming a motocross expert and you'll be on the fast track to being a better, safer and faster racer. You'll be ready to handle anything the weather, the track or your competition throw at you. You'll also know the best places to ride, the safety kit you need and much more.

ANNOY YOUR FRIENDS, THEN HELP THEM
Tune up your motocross skills by reading this book and you'll be passing your friends on the track before you know it. Of course, you'll probably want to share with them the tricks and tips you've learned – eventually. But it's very satisfying to beat someone a couple of times before you tell them what they were doing wrong!

FYI!
These features are scattered throughout the book. They contain information you can casually drop into conversation to amaze, astound, and impress your friends.

The secrets of motocross can be yours. All you have to do is read on!

4

SAVE CASH

Crashing costs money in broken bits and ripped kit. By becoming an instant motocross expert you're bound to save cash. Who knows, maybe one day you might also win some prize money?

FINDING THE RIGHT INFO

At the back of the book there's a **Troubleshooting** section that'll help you figure out what's going wrong with your riding. Nosediving over jumps? Slipping off in turns? Falling behind at the start? **Troubleshooting** tells you where to look for the fix. Or if you know exactly what the problem is, just use the contents page or index to go straight to the relevant place.

 WATCH AN EXPERT!
Throughout the book these panels point you towards web pages where you can see the relevant skills being put into practice.

 REMEMBER!
These panels tell you one thing you should always try to remember.

 LOST FOR WORDS
look here for explanations of those tricky, technical words

Motocross bikes

When motocross began, the bikes were stripped-down road machines with knobbly tyres and race numbers painted on. Today, they're highly specialized race-bred rockets. Aside from having two wheels, an engine and some handlebars, today's bikes bear little resemblance to road-going motorbikes. So what makes motocross bikes unique?

! There are three different race classes for motocross bikes:
- **MX2 is for 125cc two-strokes and 250cc four-strokes**
- **MX1 is for 250cc two-stroke or 450cc four-stroke bikes**
- **Bikes with bigger engines race in the open class**

Race numbers on and fully prepared, this motocross bike is ready to hit the track.

ENGINES

Motocross engines have to deliver a wide spread of power with instant throttle response, so that the rider can accelerate very quickly. Most bikes use highly tuned **four-stroke** engines. A few use **two-stroke** engines instead. Two-strokes normally race against four-strokes that are twice as big, because they are roughly twice as efficient as four-strokes. For example, 125cc two-strokes race 250cc four-strokes.

SUSPENSION

With up to 330mm of suspension travel at the front and rear, motocross bikes are easily able to soak up bumps and jumps. The front forks and rear suspension can be tuned to suit an individual rider's weight, speed or riding style.

four-stroke engine that produces power every two turns of the crank shaft
two-stroke engine that produces power on each turn of the crank shaft

BRAKES

Powerful hydraulic disc brakes are fitted to both wheels of the bike, but it's the front brake that does the majority of the work when slowing the machine down. The steel discs are drilled or slotted to aid cooling and to clear dirt from the braking surface. The pads are designed to be hard wearing and grippy.

TYRES

With their deep tread patterns, motocross tyres can really grip into the dirt. They offer the rider good grip in almost all conditions. Motocross tyres come in compounds and tread patterns designed to suit anything from baked-hard clay to super-sloppy mud.

FYI!

Before 1980 all motocross bikes came with two shock absorbers on the rear instead of just one like we see today. This type of bike is now commonly known as a twin-shock.

SECRET TRICK

How can you spot if a bike has a two-stroke or four-stroke motor? The easiest way is to check the size and shape of its exhaust pipe.

1 All two-stroke machines have bulbous sections of pipe leading from the engine to the silencer. This bulge in the exhaust helps increase engine power. Its size and shape affect the bike's power characteristics.

2 The front section of a four-stroke exhaust pipe is the same width all the way. The silencer has to be much bigger compared to a two-stroke machine's, to deaden the extra exhaust noise a four-stroke motor makes.

Ken Roczen

At 13, Ken Roczen was already one of the world's most expert motocross riders. Having become junior world champion in the 85cc division, Roczen was all set to become the next big star in the MX2 world championship.

STARTING YOUNG

Born in Germany, Roczen started racing at the age of three. It soon became apparent that he was an extremely talented rider, and Roczen sped through the **amateur** ranks. In 2007 he won the 85cc Junior World Championship. In 2008 Roczen raced on full-size bikes as an amateur, but achieved little in the way of major championship success. He did, though, race well at Loretta Lynn's – the USA's biggest and most important amateur motocross event.

SUCCESS AS A PRO

Roczen turned **pro** for the 2009 season. At 14, he was too young to enter the first four rounds of the 2009 world championship. As soon as his 15th birthday came around, though, Roczen was ready to race. At his home race at the German circuit of Teutschenthal, he came second in both **motos** and took the first overall win of his Grand Prix (GP) career. Roczen also became the youngest-ever GP winner, at just 15 years and 53 days old. More GP victories followed in 2010, although a string of mechanical failures meant he had to be content with the runner-up spot in the final world championship points table.

2011 AND ONWARD

In 2011 Roczen signed to race for Red Bull-KTM, who are among the world's most powerful MX teams. Whatever success follows Roczen's move, this hard-working teenage sensation is a great example for all would-be motocross racers to follow.

FACT FILE

Name: Ken Roczen

Date of birth: April 28, 1994

Nationality: German

Height: 170cm (5' 6")

Weight: 60kg (132lb)

Residence: Mattstedt, Germany

Marital status: Single

Favourite music: Punk, Limp Bizkit, Linkin Park

Favourite food: Pizza

Favourite drink: Red Bull

Hobbies: Snowboarding

Ken's advice to young motocross riders is simple. Don't practice or train too much at a really young age – just enjoy riding. He says that it is only when you get older that you start to understand the things at which you need to train harder. In the meantime, it's best just to have fun.

FYI!

Ken's favourite pet is a huge German mastiff dog called Blacky.

Buying a used bike

Motocross bikes live a hard life. When buying a used bike, look at its general condition and try to figure out if it's been looked after. Don't be blinded by sticker kits or cool-looking parts. If the bike looks unloved, don't buy it, however cheap it seems. So which parts should you check before buying?

> **!**
>
> If you remember one thing about buying a used bike, make it:
> • **First check the engine and frame numbers (see the Secret Trick on p.11), then the condition of the bike**

This used bike looks great – but you'd need to give it a careful check-over before parting with any cash.

SPROCKETS
Look for worn or damaged **sprockets**. If the sprocket is bent or the teeth are worn unevenly so that they look like little shark fins, the sprocket and chain *both* need to be replaced.

AIRBOX
Ask the seller to take off the seat or remove the cover to let you look inside the airbox. (If they don't know how, don't buy the bike.) This area of the bike should always be spotless and the air filter should be clean and freshly oiled.

BRAKES
The braking surface of the disc should be flat and have no grooves in it. The brake pads should have at least 3mm of material left on them. Pads and discs are not too expensive or difficult to replace, but do negotiate a discount on the price if they are worn.

sprocket toothed disc on the rear wheel, which connects to the chain

ENGINE AND GEARBOX

Visually check the engine for any damage or oil leaks. Next, start it up and listen for any unusual noises or knocking, while feeling for heavy vibration. Put the bike on a stand so the rear wheel is off the ground, and run through the gears. Make sure you can select all the gears and that there are no nasty noises coming from the transmission.

SUSPENSION

Check for fluid leaks from the forks and rear suspension, then push down on the bike to compress them. Nasty noises or a clunky feel mean big repair bills are likely to be coming up soon.

FYI!

At least three manufacturers are currently developing electric-powered motocross bikes.

SECRET TRICK

It's important to check the bike you are buying isn't stolen. Buying a stolen bike can lead to you having to hand it back to the original owner, or even being prosecuted by the police.

1 Most importantly, check the engine (a) and frame (b) numbers. If they've been removed or tampered with, don't buy the bike.

2 Try to get some proof that the seller does really own the bike, as well as evidence of where he or she lives.

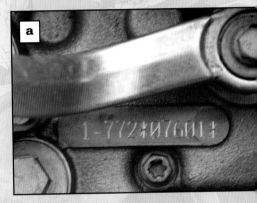

3 Ask the owner if he or she has a service book for the bike or receipts for work that has been done on it.

Riding **equipment**

If you remember one thing about buying riding kit, make it:

- **Always try it on! Sizing differs from brand to brand**

The rulebook demands racers have certain equipment. Other pieces of equipment are optional but equally important. Here's everything you need to know about protecting yourself while you're behind the (handle) bars.

HELMET AND GOGGLES

Brain injuries are extremely serious, so always protect your head with the best-quality, best-fitting helmet you can afford. Eye injuries can also be serious and permanent, so every time you hit the track make sure you are wearing good-quality goggles. When buying goggles, make sure they fit inside the eye port of your helmet and that the foam seals against your face all the way around.

BOOTS

Only ever buy specialist MX boots. Try on as many different pairs as you can and buy the ones that fit best. Ideally you're looking for some that hold your ankles snugly, but that aren't so stiff that you struggle to move your ankles. If the boots are too stiff you will find it tricky to change gears or use the rear brake.

Check out more advice on helmet fitting, by logging on to:
www.acblack.com/instantexpert

roost dirt, dust and debris thrown up by the wheels of a motocross bike

To protect your head properly a helmet needs to fit perfectly. When putting on a helmet, take hold of the two chinstraps, spread the helmet apart by pulling on the straps, then pull it over your head.

1 When the helmet's in place your eyes should be in the centre of the eye port. The padding should be in contact with your head, forehead and cheeks, but not so tight that it pinches.

PROTECTION

Body armour takes the sting out of flying **roost** and can protect your upper body, joints and limbs in crashes. The ideal armour offers maximum protection but doesn't make it hard to move around on the bike. Your knees also need protection every time you ride. Many riders use knee braces, but these can be expensive. Those who can't afford knee braces get knee pads instead.

2 To check for correct fit, get someone to try and move the helmet on your head. Rather than rolling around on your skull, the helmet should move only as much as your skin will let it.

FYI!

Fifty years ago, 'safety gear' comprised of leather pants, rugby shirts and military-style helmets.

Where to ride

If you remember one thing about riding off-road, make it:
• **Get permission to ride before firing up your bike**

You've got a bike and all the kit – now it's time to get out and do some riding! Where can you go to practise? This section will clue you in to where as well as where *not* to ride, plus giving you some tips on the best time to go riding.

FYI!

Get caught riding illegally and in some countries your bike could be crushed by the police.

Finding a practice track shouldn't be too tricky.

This landowner has made his or her feelings about off-road riders pretty clear.

WHERE NOT TO RIDE

In general it's safe to assume that you *can't* ride on a piece of land unless you have permission from the landowner or leaseholder. Public land, parks, beaches, footpaths, fields and trails are also **off-limits**. So are recognized racetracks, unless there's a race or an official practice session going on and you have permission to take part.

off-limits not available for use

FINDING A PRACTICE TRACK

The biggest and best tracks will be advertised. Check magazines and your local racing paper, as well as scouring the Internet for information. If that doesn't give you some ideas for tracks in the area that you could use, try asking your local dirt-bike dealer and other riders where they go.

GOING RACING

Most riders will find that there are at least a couple of race meetings in their local area. It's usually best to start off at these small, local meetings. If you improve enough to start winning local races, it's time to look for harder challenges further afield. If you get to a point where you can beat the fastest riders in your region, it will be time to think about racing the nationals.

SECRET TRICK

When to go riding can be as important as where you go riding. This decision depends on your level of skill and what you want to get out of your practice or training session.

1 If you're still new to MX, the morning might be the best time. You'll benefit from riding a freshly prepared track, which will be smoother, safer and much less demanding to ride. You'll be able to concentrate on applying good riding techniques rather than battling the track.

2 If you're already a motocross expert, wait until later in the day to go riding. The track will be much rougher and will offer you more of a physical challenge as you pound out your practice motos.

15

Fitness and training

Motocross is one of the most physically demanding sports there is. To get the most enjoyment out of a day at the races, you need to be in good shape. These tips will help keep training fun. There's also information on ideal types of food and how much you need to drink.

! If you remember one thing about training, make it:
• **Always do a form of physical exercise you enjoy**

Mountain biking is excellent cross-training for motocross riding.

HAVING FUN
The best training for MX is riding MX, but many people like to combine that with other activities. The key to good training is finding something that's physically demanding but still fun. You could try these for starters:

• Running is great for improving **aerobic** fitness, though it is relatively hard on the knees and ankles.

• Cycling or swimming are good activities for riders who have existing knee or ankle injuries.

• Downhill mountain biking offers a similar thrill to MX, and uses many of the same muscle groups.

• Skateboarding, snowboarding and surfing all build up fitness and are good training for your legs.

INJURIES
Motocross is a tough sport and it's not uncommon for a rider to get injured. If that happens to you, don't put a total stop to your training. Try instead to work around the injury. For instance, if you've got an upper-body injury, try cycling on a static bike.

FYI!
Scientific tests have proved that professional motocross racers are among the fittest athletes on the planet.

FUELLING THE BODY

Good diet is really important if you want to perform properly on race day. If you're training hard and racing regularly, you will need a diet that includes protein such as meat or fish, **complex carbohydrates**, calcium, vitamins and iron.

WETTER IS BETTER

If you start to **dehydrate** your strength, endurance and speed of movement will all be affected. Most people need to drink around two litres (4.2 pints) of water a day to stay in peak condition. If you're training and racing hard you'll need more than this.

STICK AT IT

The benefits of physical training take a while to become evident. When you've started training, stick at it. You'll be more than glad you did when the wins start rolling in!

aerobic with oxygen; aerobic exercise improves the performance of the heart and lungs, which circulate oxygen to the muscles
complex carbohydrate foods that provide energy and help digestion, such as brown rice, spinach, potatoes and beans
dehydrate lose fluid from the body

Accelerating

Proper acceleration is one of the most overlooked skills in motocross. Learning to accelerate well is *guaranteed* to lower your lap times. There's a lot more to it than just opening the throttle as wide as possible! Body position and clutch control are equally important.

! If you remember one thing about accelerating, make it:
- **Be sure you're in the correct position on the bike *before* you open the throttle**

THE BASICS

Whether you're opening the throttle after coming out of a corner or landing from a jump, get your body position correctly balanced before accelerating. If you're too far forward the rear wheel is likely to lose grip. If you're too far back your bike may get too much grip and could **loop out**. It's important to stay central on the bike at all times, so that you're ready to make quick adjustments when necessary.

THE ATTACK POSITION

Whether sitting or standing there are certain body-position guidelines you should follow that will help you maximize bike control. Your head should always be above the handlebar clamps while you look forward towards upcoming obstacles. Your elbows should be high, your knees bent – but still carrying your weight – and your back arched slightly forward. This is known as the **attack position**.

SECRET TRICK

How do you keep your right elbow high, in the attack position, when you're opening the throttle all the way? The secret is to use the over-grip procedure.

1 To pull the over-grip off like a pro you need to rotate your wrist away from your body and grip the throttle in an exaggerated off position.

CLUTCH CONTROL

Whenever you are riding you should have one or two fingers covering the clutch lever. This is particularly important when accelerating. You can pull in the clutch slightly to get the engine up to speed if it is struggling in too high a gear. Similarly if your front wheel lifts because you have too much traction you can momentarily pull in the clutch to regain control.

attack position optimum riding position when accelerating or approaching obstacles
loop out crash caused when the front wheel comes up so high that the rider falls off the back of the bike
throttle twist-grip on right-hand side of handlebar that controls acceleration

FYI!

Motocross bikes are geared to accelerate quickly from corner to corner, rather than for a high top speed.

2 If you start in this position, when you twist the throttle backward to accelerate, your wrist will be in line with your arm. This gives maximum control.

Braking

> If you remember one thing about braking, make it:
> • **Once your body is in the correct position, squeeze the brakes on smoothly**

The quicker you can ride your bike in a straight line the better you'll need to be at braking – otherwise you'll have a tough time turning! These top tips will have you slowing down your dirt bike more quickly and safely than ever before.

THE BASICS

Slowing down your motocross bike safely means much more than simply applying both brakes. As with all other riding skills, having the correct body position is vital. For braking, the stance you need to adopt is similar to the standard attack position. Just lean a little further back, to move your weight toward the rear of the bike. This will balance the bike as you are slowing down rapidly. The rear wheel will be kept planted on the ground.

USING THE BRAKES

Your front brake does most of the actual work of slowing your bike down. The rear brake also plays an important part, however. It keeps the bike in a straight line and stops the rear wheel from lifting off the ground. Apply the brakes smoothly, rather than immediately braking as hard as possible. Avoid **locking up** the front wheel, and if the front wheel does start to skid, release the brake momentarily while you regain control.

SECRET TRICK

You'd be surprised how many racers have their front brake lever set up so it's more tiring and difficult to use than it needs to be. This leads to the rider relying on the less effective rear brake late in the moto, as his or her arms tire.

1 Slacken the lever off on the adjuster. This will cause the brake to work much closer to the handlebar grip than it did previously.

PICK THE RIGHT LINE

While trying to position yourself on the track for an obstacle or turn, try and choose a **line** that avoids slick spots, stones, or anything else that could cause the tyres to slip. If they do slip, it will have a negative effect on your bike's ability to slow down safely and effectively.

line specific route or direction of travel followed by a bike
locking up skidding

2 Make sure that your fingers do not have to bend downward or upward to grip the brake lever. It (and the clutch lever) should be in line with your forearm. If they are not, get an expert mechanic to adjust them for you. These adjustments will give you more control over the machine and put less strain on your hand and forearm muscles.

FYI!

As well as slowing a bike, the rear brake can be used to change the bike's position in mid-air during a jump (see page 32 for more information).

Basic
cornering

Flat turns on a motocross track come in all sorts of curves and configurations, but the basic technique for getting around them is pretty much always the same. Turns are another part of riding skills in which body position plays the most important part.

!

If you remember one thing about basic turning technique, make it:
• **Sit down on the seat to lower your centre of gravity**

ENTERING THE TURN

Body position is super-important when changing direction on your motocross bike. For flat turns you need to lower your centre of gravity as much as possible. This means sitting down on the bike's saddle when you've finished braking. Slide to the front of the seat as you enter the corner, stick out your inside leg and start to put some pressure on the outside footpeg. Raise your outside elbow and hold your body as close to 90° as possible to the ground, while sitting on the outside edge of the seat.

THE MIDWAY POINT

As you reach the **apex** of the turn, steadily start to open the throttle. Keep your body nice and relaxed to help soak up any bumps, but keep the body position described in 'Entering the Turn', above. Selecting a smooth line through the turn will lessen any chances of the tyres losing grip and allow you to keep as much speed as possible.

POWERING AWAY

As you're nearing the exit of the turn you should already be looking forward at the next obstacle. Open the throttle to accelerate away at top speed, and concentrate on applying the acceleration techniques from page 18. Don't forget to put your inside foot back on the footpeg!

> **apex** tightest part of a turn
> **brake slide** skid done deliberately to turn the bike quicker in a corner

Want to see someone putting basic cornering techniques into practice?
Then check out:
www.acblack.com/instantexpert

SECRET TRICK

Although you should do the majority of your braking before entering a corner, there are times when it's necessary to use the brakes in the turn itself.

1 If you find yourself carrying too much speed through a turn, drag the rear brake slightly. This will stop the front wheel from losing traction.

2 Locking up the rear wheel with the back brake midway through a turn causes the bike to do a small **brake slide**. You can use this to change direction more quickly.

Advanced **cornering**

If you remember one
thing about cornering
control, make it:
• **Keep your eyes focused
on where you want to go,
not the ground under your
front wheel**

**Once you've mastered the
basics of changing direction
on your dirt bike, you're
ready to learn some advanced
cornering techniques. This
means it's time to take on**
ruts **and** berms. **These little
channels and dirt banks can
make a new rider's life a
complete misery.**

RUTS
The key thing to know about ruts is that as
soon as your wheels are in one, the rut is in
charge of your direction. All you can control
is your speed. Relax, ride with the rut and

you'll be fine. One common mistake riders
make is to look down at their front wheel,
then try to steer their way through the rut.
This usually leads to the rider overbalancing
and crashing. Instead, keep looking forward

BERMS
Berms are less tricky to ride through than
rutted turns and can be great places to make

up time on the competition. The way to do this
is to get your braking done before the turn,
line up your wheels, slide your weight forward

SECRET TRICK

Sometimes corner ruts get so deep that your foot controls (the brake pedal on the right or gear lever on the left) dig into them. Chances are you won't notice this happening until your bike mysteriously changes gear by itself, your gear lever gets torn off, or the brake pedal gets bent around so far that you can't use it.

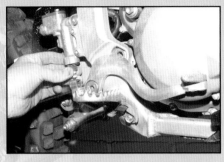

1 When you're next racing at a heavily rutted racetrack, adjust the gear and brake levers so they're higher.

2 Most riders move the foot controls so they're higher than the top of the footpeg. This gives more ground clearance and makes it less likely they will get bent or knocked off.

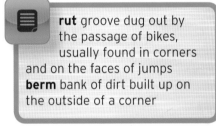

rut groove dug out by the passage of bikes, usually found in corners and on the faces of jumps

berm bank of dirt built up on the outside of a corner

at all times. Make sure both wheels are in line as you enter the rut, then follow the normal cornering rules. If you do this properly the rut will guide you around the corner and you'll be accelerating away in no time.

Want to see how to adjust your foot controls for deep ruts? Check out: www.acblack.com/instantexpert

on the seat, and then lean in with your inside leg forward and your outside elbow high. Just before you get to the apex of the turn

you should be able to open the throttle quite aggressively, as the banked side of the berm will allow your tyres a little extra grip.

Starts

Motocross races can't be won at the start – but they can definitely be lost. Grab the holeshot and you can control the pace from the front. Get away from the start badly and you'll have to fight your way past a lot of other riders in order to win. Here's everything you need to know about getting off the start line fast.

! If you remember one thing about starts, make it:
• **Keep your weight forward as you leave the start gate**

Getting a good start gives you a great chance of winning the whole race.

FYI!
In the days before metal start gates were invented, elastic bungee cords were used to control the start of races.

BODY POSITION
At the start line, sit as far forward on the bike as you can. Have both feet down on the ground, in front of the footpegs. Lean forward with your elbows up and your head over the handlebars. When the 5-second board is turned to signal 5 seconds to go until the start, select second (not first) gear, open the throttle about halfway, and feed out the clutch so it's starting to **bite**. Now watch the gate.

bite engage and pull the bike forward
holeshot first place at the first corner of a race
powershift change up a gear at full throttle and without using the clutch

LEAVING THE LINE

As the starting gate drops, release the clutch and open the throttle fully. The bike will want to wheelie, so keep your weight over the bars to ensure that you keep control. As you power away, move your feet back to the pegs in time for the all-important change into third gear. Move backward in the saddle to maximize grip.

MISSION ACCOMPLISHED?

If you've done everything right, you should have your handlebars in front of everyone else's at this point. Your throttle stays fully open as you **powershift** up through the gears on your way to the first turn. Brake as late as you can for the corner, and pick the smoothest line. Make the turn as quickly as possible – you definitely don't want to waste all your hard work and let another racer past.

SECRET TRICK

You might have the best starting technique and fastest bike in the world, but you're not going to take the holeshot if the spot you're starting from isn't properly prepared.

1 All starting gates have a rut in them, worn by the last racer's back tyre. Prepare the rut by kicking it into shape so it's nice and straight. Remove any loose dirt or stones, then stamp down the soil to maximize the back tyre's grip.

2 The photo above shows a well-prepared starting spot, which will give the rider a good start. The rut to the right of it has been left untouched from the moto before, and will produce a slow start.

Supercross

Big air, killer whoops and bar-to-bar battles – supercross is thrill-a-minute indoor motocross racing. It is rapidly gaining popularity around the world. As a result, there's a pretty good chance that a supercross event will be happening at a stadium near you soon.

EARLY DAYS OF SUPERCROSS

Dirt bikes were first raced inside a stadium in mid-1950s Czechoslovakia. The race was part of the country's Great Victory Day celebrations. However, it was in the USA that supercross first really took off. In the summer of 1972 a race was held in the Los Angeles Coliseum in California. Since then the sport has grown and grown, to the point where it now regularly packs out football and baseball stadiums around the world.

AMERICAN MOTORCYCLIST ASSOCIATION SUPERCROSS

The American Motorcyclist Association (AMA) supercross championship begins each January and runs until May. This is the biggest supercross race series in the world, and has produced famous riders such as Bob 'Hurricane' Hannah, Jeremy 'Showtime' McGrath and Ricky 'the GOAT' Carmichael. Supercross stars are adored by the public and earn a fortune in prize money and sponsorship deals. The 2007 and 2009 champion James 'Bubba' Stewart even stars in his own reality TV show!

SUPERCROSS AROUND THE WORLD

Supercross is now popular all round the world, particularly in Australia and Europe.

● Australia's national championship series is currently co-promoted by Chad Reed. Reed is a multi-time world, American and Australian supercross champion. The Australian series runs in the later half of the year, and the competition is so good that many American riders use it as a warm-up for the AMA series.

● Europe has many supercross events, with Spain, France, Germany and the UK all having successful domestic championships of their own during the winter months.

There are so many jumps at a supercross race that it sometimes seems the riders spend more time in the air than they do on the track.

FYI!

With 72 victories to his name, Jeremy McGrath has won more supercross events than any other rider in the history of the sport.

Basic
jumping

Jumping a motocross bike is one of the most enjoyable feelings you can experience. The good news is that jumping isn't actually all that difficult. However, it can be very dangerous, so it's important to learn techniques carefully and always ride within your limits.

! If you remember one thing about jumps, make it:
• **Start small, and only move to bigger jumps when you're 100% confident**

THE APPROACH
Small jumps are perfect for learning how your bike reacts in the air. When learning jump techniques, always start small and work your way up to bigger jumps. When approaching the jump, always make sure you're central on the bike so you're not affecting its overall balance. The faster you hit a jump the higher and further you go. Always make sure you know what's on the other side of the jump before taking off, and where you want to land.

TAKING OFF
As you ride up the face of the jump, keep the throttle on while maintaining the attack position. As you leave the ramp, slowly ease off the throttle and lean back slightly. This will prevent the rear end of the bike lifting as the suspension. **decompresses**. Stay relaxed and focused.

AIRTIME
Stay central on the bike as you fly through the air, but be ready to lean forwards or backwards to help keep the bike level. Stay focused on your landing spot, and get ready to return to the ground.

FYI!
In 2008, Ryan Capes did the longest ever jump by a rider on a motocross bike. He jumped 118.9m (390ft).

decompress expand or stretch out
nosedive where the front wheel is too low during a jump

SECRET TRICK

If you find yourself flying through the air with the front wheel lower than the rear, you are in a **nosedive** situation. There are a couple of things you can do to avoid a nasty crash.

1 Pull back on the bars and lean right back on the bike. Chances are this won't completely sort out the problem, in which case you will need to try step two.

LANDING

As you come in to land, stay in a central position but be ready to soak up some of the force of the landing with your knees and elbows. Landing with the throttle partially open and the rear wheel driving helps the suspension work properly and softens the impact of landing.

2 Open the throttle quickly in mid-air. This will increase the speed at which the rear wheel is spinning, which in turn causes it to drop.

Advanced jumping

Complicated jumps such as tabletops **and** doubles **require more skill than small, simple jumps. You have to time the jump so that you land perfectly on the landing ramp, with both wheels hitting the dirt at exactly the same time.**

If you remember one thing about advanced jumps, make it:

• **Don't jump tabletops or doubles before you're an expert at changing the angle of the bike in the air**

FYI!

Advanced jumping techniques were first developed in the mid-1980s, by Honda team riders David Bailey and Rick Johnson.

TIMING AND SPEED
To time a jump perfectly, you have to get your approach speed right. This will allow you to jump just the right distance to hit the landing area. Nobody can tell you how fast to go for a particular jump, it's something you learn with time. Build up your experience steadily. Before you try a big, dangerous double, for example, get the technique right on a smaller, simpler tabletop.

APPROACH AND TAKE OFF
Approach the jump in the normal attack position and at the correct speed. As you hit the face of the jump absorb some of the impact with your knees and elbows, accelerate up the ramp and then slowly turn off the throttle as you leave the ground.

SECRET TRICK

What do you do if you're flying through the air with the front wheel way too high? Don't panic - there's actually a top trick that might just get you out of trouble.

1 Moving from your central position on the bike, shift your weight forwards.

2 As you do this, pull in the clutch and tap the back brake pedal with your foot.

These actions will bring down the front end, allowing you to race on like a motocross hero.

AIRTIME

Adjust the angle of the bike with your body as you take off, remembering that you want to land with both wheels together on the **backside** of the jump. When you leave the ramp the bike's front wheel will be slightly high. Shifting your weight forwards should level it off.

HAPPY LANDINGS

Before you start lowering the front of the bike, ready to land both wheels together on the backside of the jump, make sure you *are* going to land on the backside. If you're too short or too long, you'll need to keep the front end high so that the rear suspension can soak up the force of the landing. If you're heading for the backside, get ready to soak up some of the landing with your knees and elbows. Land with the throttle partially on and power away.

backside downward-sloping landing area of a jump

double pair of jumps positioned so that it's possible to jump from the first and land on the backside of the second

tabletop jump similar to a double but with the gap between the two peaks filled in

Extreme conditions

If you remember one thing about riding in extreme conditions, make it:
• **Prepare yourself and your bike well**

Motocross is already a hazardous and tough sport, but occasionally extreme weather or track conditions make it even harder. The two things you need when this happens are perfect preparation and a positive mental attitude.

MUD

When it's been raining heavily and the track's a muddy mess, don't be dismayed. Prepare yourself and your bike to last the full race distance, then go all out to take the lead from the start of the race. That way you can control the race from the front, and mud from other people's tyres won't be sprayed up into your face. A small towel tucked in your trousers will allow you to clean your grips and gloves if you do crash.

SAND

Sand races are notoriously tough on your bike and your body. You need to be as fit as possible. Your bike should be prepared as carefully and completely as it can be (see pages 40 and 41). Ride smoothly as this will keep your overall speed as high as possible at all times. It's likely there will be lots of roost, so pay a bit of extra attention to making sure your goggles are perfectly clean and fit really well.

SECRET TRICK

This trick will help you keep your goggles clean for long periods of time in a mud or sand race.

1 Tape an old goggle lens to the top of your helmet peak to make the visor longer. This clear extension helps deflect roost away from your face and goggles but can still be seen through so it won't affect your vision.

HEAT

It's always important to stay well hydrated, but take extra care over this if conditions are hot and humid. You will need to drink more fluid than usual. Keep as cool as possible between motos by hanging out in the shade, or inside a vehicle with the air conditioning on a cold setting. Wear lightweight **vented** racewear and damp it down with water before your race so it keeps you cool.

2 This trick also works well if you find that a low sun is blinding you – in this instance use a tinted lens to act as a sun shield.

 handguard plastic shield fitted in front of a motorbike's hand controls for warmth and safety

vented with gaps that allow air to flow through

COLD

Thermal underwear will help keep your body warm when racing in chilly temperatures. Big **handguards**, rubber undergloves and waterproof thermal socks will help keep your hands and feet more comfortable.

Be a **pro mechanic**

Not everyone in life is cut out to be a pro racer – but there are plenty of other jobs available in motocross. If you're good with tools, know motocross bikes inside out and don't mind working long unsociable hours, maybe you could become a professional mechanic?

FYI!

Top mechanics can strip a motocross bike back to the bare frame in less than 20 minutes.

HELPING OUT FRIENDS

Most pro motocross mechanics start out by helping out a friend at a big event. This offers real excitement when all the mechanic's hard work results in good race results out on the track. Mechanics who turn out their rider's bikes immaculately race after race, suffer no **DNF**s and can work well under pressure may be offered a job on a pro team.

A WEEK IN THE LIFE OF A PRO MECHANIC

Like the idea of being a pro mechanic? Here's a typical mechanic's week during the racing season.

Monday morning: the cleanup from yesterday's race starts. There are two bikes to wash off, as well as the team truck and awning.

Tuesday to Friday: these four days pass in a blur of stripping bikes, rebuilding them, doing laundry, testing equipment, making adjustments, and preparing two race bikes for the weekend's action.

Saturday: loading the truck and travelling to the track, then putting the two race bikes through technical control, an official checkover.

Sunday, race day: an early start. After qualifying, you clean and prepare the bike for the first moto and get it to the start on time. After 'pit boarding' your rider through the moto (using boards to pass on lap times, race position and messages of encouragement) it's immediately time to clean, fix and prepare the bike for moto two. When the racing's done for the day, load up the truck before heading home.

DNF short for 'did not finish'

37

For cleaning your bike you'll need:

- **Water**
- **Power washer**
- **Exhaust bung and airbox cover**
- **Spray-on detergent**
- **Soft brush or sponge**

Cleaning your bike

Getting your motocross bike dirty is a lot more fun than washing it off afterwards! Even so, this needs to be done after every ride. Here are some top bike-washing tips that'll stop this chore from becoming too much of a bore.

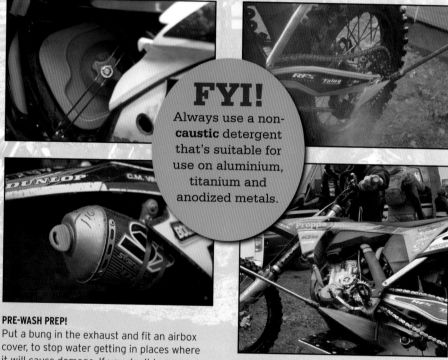

FYI!
Always use a non-**caustic** detergent that's suitable for use on aluminium, titanium and anodized metals.

PRE-WASH PREP!
Put a bung in the exhaust and fit an airbox cover, to stop water getting in places where it will cause damage. If you don't have an exhaust bung, a rag or sponge will fill the gap. If you don't have an airbox cover, see the secret trick on page 39. (Always remember to take the bung back out once you've finished cleaning!)

GET THE WORST DIRT OFF
Use a power washer and blast off the worst of the dirt. Find someone to tip the bike over so you can clean underneath the frame rails, engine and suspension linkage. Never spray high-pressure water directly at seals, gaskets, radiators or bearings. Remember to spin the wheels to make sure they're clean from every angle.

GET OUT THE SOAP AND SCRUB

When the bike appears to be dirt-free, spray plenty of detergent all over it. Leave it to soak in for a moment, then start agitating the soapy bubbles with a soft brush or sponge. Pay extra attention to areas where there are stubborn stains.

RINSE THE BIKE

When the detergent has had a chance to work, use the washer again to rinse off all the suds. Make sure the brake discs and pads get an especially good rinse clean, because some detergents affect brake-pad performance. Finally, use a water-dispersing lubricant on bare metals and moving parts, to stop them rusting or seizing up.

caustic able to corrode (eat away) metallic surfaces

SECRET TRICK

If you don't have an airbox cover there's an old trick that will keep your filter dry while you wash your bike down.

1 Unbolt your seat and take out your air filter.

2 Fit a polythene carrier bag over your air filter, tucking the handle end of the bag up inside the filter.

3 Put the filter back in place, then tighten up the mounting bolt through the bag until the filter's sealed in place. Now you can wash your bike safe in the knowledge that your filter's fully protected from water and detergent.

Want to see how to wash your bike like a pro? Check out:
www.acblack.com/instantexpert

Pre-ride **preparations**

To prepare your bike you'll need:

- **Screwdrivers**
- **8 and 10mm T-bar socket wrenches**
- **Allen keys**
- **Spoke wrench**
- **Air-filter service kit**
- **Chain lube**
- **Grease**

You might be in great physical shape. You may know all the essential riding techniques. There may be an awesome race bike parked in your garage. All this will count for nothing if your bike isn't running well. Here are some essential bike-preparation tips to carry out regularly.

FRONT-TO-BACK SAFETY CHECK
Starting from the front wheel, check that every nut and bolt is tight. Starting at the front and working backwards means you can't forget anything. Give each bolt a tweak to check it's tight and if it's not, tighten it up. If you're not sure how tight a bolt should be, consult the workshop manual that came with the bike.

FYI!

Not looking after your bike not only increases your chances of a DNF in a race, it also makes the bike worth much less when you come to sell it.

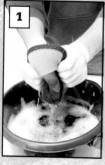

1

2

3

4

AIR FILTER
At least once a week, remove the filter, take it off the cage and clean it in **solvent**. Squeeze out all excess solvent and wash the filter in hot soapy water. Hang up the filter to dry in the air. When it's dry, inspect the filter for damage. If it's okay, put the filter in a bag and pour in some filter oil. Work the oil in until the

CHAIN - LUBRICATE AND CHECK

Lubricate your chain with off-road-specific oil. Check chain tension by slipping three fingers between the **swingarm** and chain just to the rear of the chain slipper (the plastic strip on top of the swingarm). The chain should be tight across your fingers. If you can't fit three fingers in the gap, the chain needs to be adjusted.

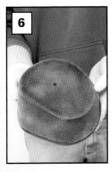

filter is covered. Squeeze out any excess oil, and replace the filter on the cage. Finally, apply a thin coat of grease to the sealing surface and reinstall the filter on the bike.

SECRET TRICK

Most riders can do basic work on their bike for themselves. Even experts, though, often leave more complicated servicing, such as oil changes and engine-part replacement, to a mechanic.

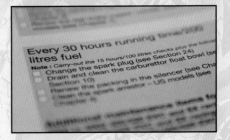

1 Use your workshop manual to know when the manufacturer recommends work should be done on the bike. This is usually needed after a set number of hours of use.

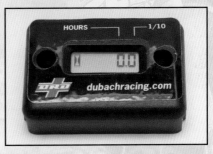

2 It's surprisingly difficult to keep an exact track of hours an engine has been used. One way to do this is to fit an **aftermarket** hour meter to your bike. Inexpensive to buy and easy to fit, this small part lets you know exactly how long your engine's been running.

aftermarket replacement or additional part
solvent liquid cleaner that removes dirt
swingarm metal arm connecting rear wheel to frame of bike

Troubleshooting

There are many elements to motocross, which is partly why it is one of the toughest sports around. Don't worry if you're struggling to get something perfect, because even the best riders occasionally get things wrong. Here are some problems racers commonly encounter, plus some possible solutions.

PROBLEM 1: STRUGGLING IN RUTS

If you're wobbling around rutted turns you need to relearn these key skills:
• Look to the end of the rut rather than down at your front wheel
• Slide up to the front of the seat when you enter the corner, with your inside leg out
• Don't fight the rut - let it guide you and your bike around the turn
• Put a little weight on the outside footpeg to make sure the tyres are biting in
• Accelerate through the rut once you've ridden past the tightest part of the turn.

PROBLEM 3: DIFFICULTY WITH JUMPS

If you're out of control over jumps try the following:
• If you're struggling with a particular jump, it might just be because you're just not ready for it yet. Go back to practicing your technique on smaller jumps such as small tabletops
• Ensure you keep a neutral body position on the bike as you approach the jump
• Make sure your speed is sufficient to clear the gap - once you're off the ground there's nothing you can do to speed up or slow down
• Be ready to pull in the clutch and tap the back brake to bring the front end down, or open the throttle to bring the rear end down.

PROBLEM 2: SLOW AT STARTS

Slow out of the start? It could be time to check your technique isn't slipping:
• Watch the part of the gate that moves first when the starter drops it
• Start with both feet down so your body is balanced as you leave the line
• Feed out the clutch smoothly but quickly
• Make sure you're opening the throttle fully
• Adjust your body position so you're getting the maximum possible amount of grip without the front wheel lifting.

PROBLEM 4: SLOW THROUGH BERMS

If you're having trouble making it around banked bends, think about these key points:

• Get your braking done before you enter the corner. If you're coming in too fast, not even perfect turning technique will get you around
• Line up your wheels as you enter the turn
• Slide up to the front of the seat and put your inside leg out
• Turn in hard and commit to the bend
• Keep looking forward
• Open the throttle when you're past the tightest part of the bend
• Accelerate away as quickly as possible.

FYI!

Even pro riders usually have a coach whose job is to help them perfect their technique.

PROBLEM 5: BIKE PROBLEMS

If your bike isn't running well it's normally because it hasn't been properly prepared:

• Whenever you wash your bike, cover the air filter and put a bung in the exhaust
• If your air filter is dirty or over-oiled, your engine won't breathe properly. Service this item correctly at least once a week – more often if you ride in dusty or sandy conditions
• Nothing ruins a race like having your seat or something else fall off. Check all the bike's bolts are tight by doing regular front-to-back bolt checks.

Technical motocross **language**

aerobic with oxygen; aerobic exercise improves the performance of the heart and lungs, which circulate oxygen to the muscles

aftermarket replacement or additional part

amateur person who does an activity without pay

apex tightest part of a turn

attack position optimum riding position when accelerating or approaching obstacles

backside downward-sloping landing area of a jump

berm bank of dirt built up on the outside of a corner

bite engage and pull the bike forward

brake slide skid done deliberately to turn the bike quicker in a corner

caustic able to corrode (eat away) metallic surfaces

complex carbohydrate foods that provide energy and help digestion, such as brown rice, spinach, potatoes and beans

decompress expand or stretch out

dehydrate lose fluid from the body

DNF short for 'did not finish'

double pair of jumps positioned so that it's possible to jump from the first and land on the backside of the second

four-stroke engine that produces power every two turns of the crank shaft

handguard plastic shield fitted in front of a motorbike's hand controls for warmth and safety

holeshot first place at the first corner of a race

line specific route or direction of travel followed by a bike

locking up skidding

loop out crash caused when the front wheel comes up so high that the rider falls off the back of the bike

moto single round of a motocross event

nosedive situation where the front wheel is too low during a jump

off-limits not available for use

powershift change up a gear at full throttle and without using the clutch

pro professional, a person paid to do an activity

roost dirt, dust and debris thrown up by the wheels of a motocross bike

rut groove dug out by the passage of bikes, usually found in corners and on the faces of jumps

solvent liquid cleaner that removes dirt

sprocket toothed disc on the rear wheel, which connects to the chain

swingarm metal arm connecting rear wheel to frame of bike

tabletop jump similar to a double but with the gap between the two peaks filled in

throttle twist-grip on right-hand side of handlebar that controls acceleration

two-stroke engine that produces power on each turn of the crank shaft

vented with gaps that allow air to flow through

Further information

BOOKS

Pro Motocross & Off-Road Riding Techniques Donnie Bales (Motorbooks, 2004)
The third edition of this book has plenty of top tips and techniques that'll help all riders out on the track.

World Sports: Dirt Biking Paul Mason (A & C Black Publishers, 2011)
This excellent little book is aimed at teenaged riders, and features suggestions for dream dirt-bike destinations around the world.

DVDs

Sometimes it's easier to pick up a technique if you're actually shown how to do it:

Stefan Everts MX Training & Racing Techniques (Duke Video, 2010)
There are currently two DVDs from 10-time MX world champion Everts – one concentrates on sand-riding techniques and the other on hard-packed soil.

Transworld Motocross: Skills (X-Treme Video, 2007)
Transworld Motocross is the world's biggest selling MX magazine and the Skills range of DVDs is very popular.

WEBSITES

www.dirtbikerider.com
This site has a social networking area called Dirtzone. This is a Facebook-friendly portal that allows you to communicate with motocross riders from around the world. You can offer and ask for advice, or just show off your riding pics and video clips.

www.motocross-racing-tips.com
www.motoxschool.com
Both these sites have lots of great advice on riding and maintaining a MX bike.

Motocross timeline

1885
Gottlieb Daimler invents and builds the world's first petrol-engined motorcycle in Schorndorf, Germany.

1924
The Southern Scott Scramble - the first-ever official motocross race - is held in Camberley, Surrey. The winner, Arthur Sparks, wins the 50-mile epic in a time of two hours, one minute and 51 seconds.

1947
Holland hosts the first ever *Motocross des Nations*, which is won by the British team made up of Bill Nicholson, Bob Ray and Fred Rist.

1952
The *Fédération International de Motocyclisme* (FIM) introduces a European championship for riders with 500cc machines. It is won by Belgium's Victor Leloup.

1956
80,000 excited Czechoslovakians pack out the Strahov stadium in Prague to witness the first-ever stadium motocross race. The race is just a small part of the Great Victory Day celebrations but is reported to be a favourite with spectators.

1957
The 500cc European series is upgraded to World Championship status. 'Super-Swede' Bill Nilsson wins the title - a feat he repeats in 1960.

1962
Thorsten Hallman - another 'Super-Swede' and the creator of the THOR clothing brand - wins the inaugural 250cc World Championship.

1970
Joel Robert powers to victory in the 250cc championship for Suzuki - the first time a Japanese manufacturer wins the world title.

1971
Bruce Brown's documentary *On Any Sunday*, starring Steve McQueen, helps introduce the American public to motocross.

1972
Modern supercross is born when the first Superbowl of Motocross is held in the Los Angeles Coliseum. Around 30,000 race fans head to the home of the 1932 and 1984 Olympic Games to witness 16-year-old Yamaha rider Marty Tripes take the overall victory.

1973
Yamaha introduce the revolutionary monoshock system on their 250cc factory bike, with a single shock absorber. This new system not only works more efficiently but also saves weight over the traditional twin-shock system.

1974
'Flying Dutchman' Pierre Karsmakers becomes the first ever AMA supercross champion. From its beginning in 1974 the American supercross series grows and grows to the point where it now regularly fills NFL stadiums across America.

1975
A third official world championship motocross category is formed, for competitors on 125cc machines. Belgium's Gaston Rahier takes the title in the championship's first year - the first of three world titles he will win.

strokes in a newly formed MXGP class. The 500cc class becomes the 650cc class and mixes 500cc two-strokes with four-stroke machines up to 650cc, while the 125cc class is opened up to riders on 250cc four-stroke machines. Belgian riders take all three titles, with Stefan Everts winning the MXGP crown, Joel Smets the 650s and Steve Ramon the 125s. Ramon's win on a KTM will be the last for a two-stroke-engined bike.

1981

Team USA takes victory in the *Motocross des Nations* by dominating in the deep sands of Lommel, Belgium. The team of Donnie Hansen, Chuck Sun, Danny LaPorte and Johnny O'Mara starts a 13-year win streak for the American nation – the longest in the history of the event.

1983

Brake technology takes a huge leap forward as Kawasaki release their production KX250 and KX500 models with a front disc brake. Until this point all bikes had been fitted with drum brakes, which were erratic performers at best – especially in the wet.

1993

After 27 years of two-stroke dominance, Belgium's Jacky Martens wins the 1993 500cc world championship on a bike with a four-stroke engine.

1997

Yamaha enter a high-revving four-stroke race machine into the AMA supercross series and 500cc world motocross championships. The radical factory YZ400M is a success and a production version – the YZ400F – is launched for the public one year later.

2003

The FIM allows 450cc four-stroke machines to race against 250cc two-

2004

The world championships receive another revamp. The MXGP class is now known as MX1, the 125 division MX2 and the 650 class MX3.

2006

Two of the greatest racers retire from full-time competition. Belgium's Stefan Everts bows out with 10 world titles and 101 GP wins to his name, while US motocross and supercross sensation Ricky Carmichael ends his career with 16 American national titles and 144 overall wins to his name in AMA competition. Despite being retired, Carmichael notches up another six major wins in 2007 to take his all-time total to 150.

2008

The 2008 model RM-Z450 is the first production motocross bike to feature electronic fuel injection. The new system increases power and makes the motor easier to start when stalled. Steve Ramon narrowly misses capturing the MX1 world title on his factory RM-Z450 after a year-long battle with David Philippaerts.

2009

Germany's Ken Roczen becomes the youngest GP winner in motocross history, winning his home round of the world championship at Teutschenthal aged just 15 years and 53 days.

Index